How to Beat the Hell Out of your Competition
(Using Customer Service)

How to Beat the Hell out of your Competition

M. A. Sharrieff

How to Beat the Hell Out of your Competition
(Using Customer Service)

M. A. Sharrieff

Published by Write On e-Publishing, LLC
for
Write On Press

How to Beat the Hell out of your Competition

M. A. Sharrieff

How to Beat the Hell Out of your Competition
(Using Customer Service)

By
M.A. Sharrieff

Published by Write On Press

Copyright 2012 Write On E-Publishing, LLC

~~***~~

All Write On E-Publishing books are sold DRM-free without copy protection or encryption. This book is licensed for your personal enjoyment only. This book may not be re-sold or given away to other people. If you would like to share this book with another person, please purchase an additional copy for each recipient. If you're reading this book and did not purchase it, or it was not purchased for your use only, then please return to your preferred book retailer and purchase your own copy. Thank you for respecting the hard work of this author.

~~***~~

Table of Contents

About this Book	7
About the Author	9
Customer Service as a Marketing Tool	10
Obtaining Market Research through Customer Service	14
Differentiation through Customer Service	17
Customer Service and Corporate Culture	25
Building Lifetime Customer Value	28
Generating New Sales through Customer Service	31
Customer Complaints as Business Opportunities	33
Maximizing Human Capital	36
Customer Service Driven Growth Strategies	44
Customer Service Trends	46
Conclusion	48
More about the Author	51

~~***~~

M. A. Sharrieff

How to Beat the Hell Out of your Competition
(Using Customer Service)

About this book

I love this title! I sincerely hope the image of beating the hell out of your market rivals using the weapon of customer service inspired you to read this book as much as it inspired me to write it. I like the idea of customer service as a real, tangible business tool that can be used to separate your business from the pack and create real profitability.

Note: Please don't abduct and literally beat the hell out of your competitors! It is illegal in most places.

I chose customer service because in my experience, it is a tool too often overlooked. It is an aspect of business that is undervalued and under-appreciated. I truly feel that those companies who adopt a customer service focus in their businesses more easily rise to the top of their industries. Those competitors who can't seem to stop hemorrhaging market share are those who refuse to change how they think of customer service and its place in their business and marketing strategy.

So, I wrote this book. But before you make the assumption that it's another of those boring business how-to's that you either can't get through, can't understand, or can't figure out how to apply the contents to your situation or business; I want you to know that this isn't one of those books. I've read dozens of those books over my years in business and most of them have been a drag, I wouldn't have the stomach to write a book like that, let alone ask you to read it.

This book is written plainly and intelligently (if I do say so myself), so that even executive management should be able to understand it. However, this book is written primarily for middle managers, call center supervisors, team leads, and customer care representatives, small and mid-sized business owners, and one-person business operations. My target audiences are those individuals who either directly interact with the customer or directly interact with those that do.

Each section is organized to quickly define the topic of discussion, offer the reason the topic is relevant, and depict the prevailing perspective and why that perspective is flawed, and how you can take advantage of the environment by shifting your own point of view. I take you directly to the paradigm that will promote and profit your business most. I've chosen not to include dozens of case studies showing how right I am because the tendency is to try to emulate exactly what the example company did to achieve success. That doesn't always work for every business model.

Instead, what I want you to do is focus on the ways in which you need to change how you think about customer service and your customer service assets. Once your vision of how customer service fits into your business changes it will be simple to devise tactics and strategies on how to use your new vision to beat the hell out of your competition using customer service.

~~***~~

About the author

So, here's why you should give a cracked walnut about anything I have to say on the subject of this book. I began my marketing career fresh out of high school in the early ninety's. Since then, I have worked for marketing firms and been a contract marketing consultant, I've worked in business management, public relations, customer service (from representative through the management level), and I've owned my own business (not including publishing a few hundred articles on a variety of business topics).

Academically, I have earned undergraduate degrees in marketing and management, a master of management and a master of business administration with an emphasis in e-commerce. I've been mentored by one of the most talented business minds in the southern United States and have had numerous opportunities to promote the biggest brands from international beer companies to the Vice President of the United States.

But beyond all that, as both a consumer and as a vendor of customer services I have paid severe attention to the foibles of businesses in regard to the use of their customer care departments over the years. I have found that within the areas outlined in this book any business leader has the power to improve their business position and eat their competitors' lunch just by shifting the way they view and use the power of customer service.

Okay, enough chit-chat! Let's get to work.

~M. A. Sharrieff

~~***~~

Customer Service as a Marketing Tool

Primer on Marketing:

Instead of jumping into the central topic of this section with the assumption that you already know everything necessary to understand how customer service can be a critical part of your company's marketing strategy, I'll start with a brief primer on marketing basics. After all, if you are reading this book it is likely that you are looking for a way to fit customer service and marketing together to benefit your organization. That's a goal that's certain to be 1000% easier with a firm grasp of some marketing fundamentals.

First you need to understand that marketing as a business practice has changed very little over the past several centuries. Oh, the tools with which we market our brands and the products and services they offer have changed significantly over the years; but make no mistake, the principles of marketing will never change as long as human psychology remains constant.

So, in brief, marketing is the communication of a benefit found within a particular product or service to a consumer or consumer group. What this means to you is that you can stop thinking of marketing as some mystical practice where suited executives employ modern day voodoo to make people buy things they don't really want (that would be politics).

Instead, know that marketing is just helping people understand that something you are selling is available and may be of particular interest to them.

Almost 2 decades ago, I found my greatest mentor. She taught me in my very first marketing class the most important tenet of the industry: *"People only ever buy two things; solutions to problems and good feelings."*

Here's what this means for you:

If you can use marketing to consistently communicate to a consumer group that what you offer will solve their problem(s) and make them feel good, then your competition would have to put forth an extreme amount of effort to derail your business' success.

Second, marketing as a practice is usually segmented into four aspects. These aspects are usually referred to as the "4-P's of Marketing."

1. Product – What you are offering the market, including services for sale and anything offered to add additional value to the core product or service.

2. Price – How much those solutions and good feelings will cost the customer and how they can make payment (terms, credit, special offers, etc.).

3. Place (or distribution) – How (conveniently) you will get the goods or services you offer to the consumer who wants to buy them.

4. Promotion – How you communicate to the prospective customer the benefits inherent in the first three aspects mentioned above.

Here's what this means for you:

Once you have settled on a product or service to offer to the market, and defined all of the benefits the offering will bring to your market, you don't have to confuse yourself with the intricacies of marketing. If you have the ability, hire a professional marketer. If you don't, you can market your products yourself. But in either case keep your marketing simple by ensuring that every strategy and marketing tactic you employ is sifted through these four filters:

1. Am I letting my target market know that I have a product that consistently delivers their desired benefits, and that those benefits are obvious and easy to obtain once they purchase from me?

2. Does my market know that my product offering is priced in a way that allows them to get a greater perceived value for their dollars spent?

3. Am I telling my customer how they can readily get their hands on my service or product; and, if there are changes in the distribution how well can I communicate this to my customer?

4. Does my promotion strategy effectively and consistently communicate to my target customer all of the relevant problems my product or service can solve and all of the good feelings it can provide to them?

Every marketing strategy and tactic that successfully gets through these filters will support your business effort.

Primer on Customer Service:

So, what is customer service exactly? From a business management perspective, customer service can be viewed as an additional service offering supporting your core product or service. If you ask your friendly neighborhood marketing professional, they'll say that customer service is a means to develop the long-term relationship between the business and its consumer. Viewed through the perspective of the consumer, customer service is a necessary tool that "should" ensure consistent delivery of the solutions and good feelings they have come to your business to purchase.

Here's what this means for you:

You need to know that 99% of the time how you service your customers before, during and after the sale will be the key aspect that determines if you can convert customer interest into a first sale and a first sale into a lifetime of profitable business transactions.

One of the facts of doing business today is that almost every market offering can be duplicated by your competition within six months of market entry. What can't be duplicated are the unique, human based aspects of your product mix. These aspects are composed of every point of contact between a "live" representative of your company and the customer.

So, if this is one of the few ways to make your brand the superior choice in the mind of your customer, significant focus and effort should be directed in developing customer service, knowing it can be the tool that helps you beat the hell out of your competition.

Using Customer Service to Market your Product, Service and Brand:

Okay, now that we've covered the basics, let's talk about how customer service can be employed to market your product or service.

First, let's debunk a few misconceptions.

Automated voice response systems that require you to press or say "one" in order to perform any function (like paying a bill or getting information) are not customer service. These are service tools; they provide no point of live contact between the customer and your business and actually result in a straining of the relationship between your business and your customer. Other service tools can include automated outbound pre-recorded calls leaving important business messages or asking your customer to call another 1-800 number. Another is the automated customer service text to deliver information or request the customer call in for additional service.

Call centers only house customer service assets (the people who provide the service); they do not offer customer service in and of themselves. Just having a call center does not mean that you are providing any level of service to your customers. Many call centers are even decentralizing and allowing representatives to telecommute from home to reduce costs and provide service from happier human assets (a trending tactic to maximize human capital).

These devices are tools. Although they are useful tools, you'll need to recognize that they do nothing to increase customer loyalty or enhance the lifetime value of the customer for your business.

Here's what this means for you:

Knowing the difference between customer service tools and the assets that actually produce customer service and enhance the consumer relationship can help you to maximize your effort to market your business as superior because of the continuous access your customer will have to solutions and good feelings. Once you've effectively communicated this marketing message to your target market, your competition can't win those customers from you unless you let them.

So, when viewing marketing as a means of communicating the benefits your offering provides to prospective customers, each of your customer service assets (representatives, team leads, managers, quality assurance, etc.) will all need to be continually focused on this effort.

Every contact with the customer will center on how your business can solve their problems. Every contact should end with the customer feeling happier about their purchase decision and the business relationship than when the contact began.

If marketing is a means of communicating how much better your product offering is for the customer than that of the competition, and if customer service is one of the premier ways of communicating your marketing message to the prospective, ongoing and veteran customer, then with a focus on the development of customer service assets who consistently solve customer problems and make your customers feel good about the business relationship you can beat the hell out of your competition.

Obtaining Market Research through Customer Service

Why do you need marketing research anyway?

Again, it might be less than considerate to assume a complete understanding of market research and its value in the development of your brand and market position. So, we'll take a minute to cover the basics.

Market research is the business intelligence gained from the qualified actual and potential customers that make up your company's target market. In essence, market research tells business leaders how, when, where, why and for how many dollars customers want their needs to be serviced.

Market research can often be one of the most expensive aspects of a company's marketing strategy, but without it you're really just flying blind. Beyond the expense, market research can be a difficult, complex endeavor, requiring boat loads of time and effort to get right.

Many small and mid-sized firms have failed because they made the choice to forego the effort needed to gain the necessary market intelligence to out-compete business adversaries. Unfortunately, they found that even though they saved money and time, their competition beat the hell out of them because they knew how to better serve their customers.

Here's what this means for you:

You need to know what your customers want and how they want it; market research answers these questions. So, you need to find the most effective, least expensive, and most expeditious method of gaining qualified market research.

So, what's the best way to connect with customers in your target market population to find out what you can do to better address their business needs? Well, since you have business representatives who interact with your customers every day, discussing how best to address customer concerns, perhaps capturing this information would be a productive first step.

Also, if your business has more than a handful of employees dedicated to customer interaction, it's likely you'll want to ensure that those interactions are of top quality by recording them and reviewing them for, "quality assurance and training purposes." Well, while you're reviewing how well the representative interacted with the customer, you can also pull relevant market research directly from the customer half of the conversation.

Encourage your representatives to ask customers, "What can I do to be of further service?" or, "What can I do to provide additional value for you?" or, "What kind of resolution would best solve this issue for you?"

Help your representatives understand how valuable the market research they can obtain for you is to the company. Reward them for their effort and participation and sell them the vision of how market research contributes to business success.

Research gained during the customer service interaction is more valuable than any you can ever buy. Not only can you save vast sums of money by obtaining your qualified market research through customer service, but you can also reinforce your customer relationships by showing how much you value your customer's input.

How do you get the best and most effective market research through customer service?

Now that you've educated your customer on how much you value their input, send them a thank you note or email as a follow up. In the correspondence ask if they know anyone who they think might also benefit from the products and services you provide. Then have them refer those individuals contact info for the express and exclusive purpose of asking their opinion on how they feel your company could best service their needs.

Once you've followed through, you've gained additional exposure to a qualified customer and got valuable market research without spending any more money than you otherwise would on similar customer service functions.

Reward your customers for their opinions and feedback with discounts on future sales. Design internal public relations campaigns that reward customer service staff for supporting the market research effort. Tactics like these will turn your customer service team and your established customer base into an army of market researchers.

Here's what this means for you:

By making some modest strategic changes in the way you implement customer service, you can obtain large amounts of qualified market research. The cost of obtaining this market intelligence will be minute compared to that of employing a professional market researcher to do surveys and focus groups. If properly done, you can increase customer loyalty, competitive positioning and even increase sales! In addition to all these benefits, you gain access to additional market share and potential expansion markets with the knowledge of how to beat the hell out of your competition already in hand!

  Sell your staff on a vision of customer service that includes gaining market research on every customer interaction. Educate your customer base on how valued their opinions and feedback are to your business. Employ strategies and tactics that encourage and reward market research referrals. Your results will likely include more and better market intelligence than you could have ever afforded to buy at little to no additional cost.

Differentiation through Customer Service

Differentiation is quite simply the act of making your business seem different (hopefully in a positive way) when compared to other competitors in the industry.

Since we already know that almost every product or service you can offer to a potential customer can be replicated for sale within about six months on average, it is likely that whatever business venture you are in, you will need a strategy that makes you unique in the mind of your target consumer.

While every tactic and strategy discussed in this book can effectively differentiate your business from your competition, all of the topics discussed have been geared toward enhancing the customer service function to include marketing, market research and other business activities normally set apart from customer service.

In this section, we'll discuss how the traditional functions of customer service can be used to make your business seem like a super star within your competitive field.

So, let's start by identifying some of the major customer service functions.
- Inbound issue resolution
- Inbound purchase or payment processing
- Outbound collections
- Outbound (response or pre-emptive) issue resolution
- General information
- Supplementary services and product sales
- Refunds, returns and exchanges

Every mid-sized and large firm in existence today will have a department of representatives dedicated to managing these functions and the detailed activities that will fall under these broader categories. Of course even in a broad sense, the list above is by no means exhaustive. All too often, business leaders fail to understand just how much of their business survival (let alone success) depends upon the effort and skill of its customer service department. So, instead of drowning in the depth of business functions performed by the average customer service representative, we'll use the list above to illustrate some pertinent examples that will offer direction in your differentiation efforts.

So, the most important, in fact the number one critical factor that can separate your business from the pack is how different your company's business perspective is from your competitors. In almost every industry you will find established market leaders and copycat followers that all share the same view of how business should be done in the industry. These market players establish the 'traditional' methods of doing business. Don't buy into it.

Every new business entering the market must decide whether to emulate the established modus operandi or take a chance on something different.

Here's the good news: when it comes to customer service, there's the established way and there's the better way.

Take some time to read the many articles, white papers and case studies on companies like Southwest Air, Zappos.com, or USAA. These companies were not established business juggernauts. They were upstart companies with a different way of thinking about customer relationships and service. What's significant is that these new ways of servicing their customers were not only successful in taking market share from their competitors (so these are proven methodologies) but in every case they are the same perspective.

Here's what this means for you:

You can try to compete with the big boys by playing the game by their rules, or you can follow the lead of companies that have already beaten the big boys of their industry by changing how the game is played.

Here are a few examples:

Inbound Issue Resolution – This is what everyone thinks of when they hear the term customer service. Its most often viewed as a 1-800 number that will lead to a representative who can help solve a problem the customer is having post-purchase.

Your competitors will view this as a customer contact where their representative needs to focus on quickly addressing the primary concern of the caller in order to prevent a return or refund situation. Business leadership will regularly pressure the customer service team to identify the key concern of the caller, resolve it and move on to the next caller in as few minutes as possible.

The representative will tell the customer how they will solve their problem, apologize profusely for any inconvenience they might have suffered and wish them a good day, all the while hoping they have not adversely affected their average call time.

Here's what this means for you:

Educate your representatives that they need to possess a sense of urgency, not so they maintain a certain metric, but because the customer wants to feel that resolving their problem is as important to you as it is to them.

Have your representative take the necessary time to understand the how the issue originated, identify the root cause and address it as well as the symptom the customer called with. Suggest ways the customer can use your product or service so they avoid any similar issues in the future.

By having your customer service assets exercise a priority to customer concern and consideration over reduction of sales returns or refunds, your consumers will be more likely to elevate your brands' competitive position in their mind.

Inbound Purchase or Payment Processing – This is the aspect of customer service that all business managers wish was the only aspect of customer service. Money, money, money, money! Keep those phones ringing and those sales totals increasing. But, again these guys totally miss an opportunity to distinguish themselves among their competitors.

Your competitors will view each inbound payment or sales call as a queue of customers stretched out before each customer service representative. That representative should be processing those incoming payments as efficiently as possible so the maximum number of sales can be recorded before the end of that business day. If anything interrupts that inflow of receipts, it must have something to do with a previously unseen ineptitude of the representative. After all, all they have to do is record sales, right?

Here's what this means for you:

Have your customer service representatives (CSRs) view each sales or payment transaction as a speed date. The customer wants to give you money, so they are already attracted to you as a potential business mate. What your CSRs need to do is establish rapport, trust, mutual concern for the development of the relationship, and an understanding of the mutual benefits that exist for them (as a business representative) and the customer in a long-term commercial association.

So when the call comes through, your CSR should understand that receipt of the payment is important but not as important as engaging the customer in a way that makes them want to call back for future sales. Returning to the two things that people buy; if the customer has already committed to solving their problem with your product or service, have your CSRs deliver a free dose of good feelings as an unexpected bonus.

Once a purchase is converted into a relationship, it'll take an extreme amount of effort for your competitors to ever get that customer to be unfaithful.

Outbound Collections - Queue up the ominous background music! Everybody hates outbound collections. Customers, CSRs, managers, even the maintenance staff hates collections! But it doesn't have to be that way.

Your competitors will consider the collections staff, queue, or department a necessary evil and a means of chasing down deadbeat customers. Their staff will adopt this attitude and deal with customers in the harsh, negative and demeaning style of a modern day leg-breaker. Believe me; customers don't like that at all. Pretty soon, your collections staff is swapping anecdotes regarding children answering the phone with, "My daddy says he isn't here."

Here's what this means for you:

Use the out bound collections call as an opportunity to strengthen trust between your business and your customer. Empower your collections staff with tools and options to help work with the customer in a variety of scenarios. Have them communicate true concern for the customer's position and a desire to help provide a solution where the needs of the customer and the business are served. Prioritize the collection of the cash after finding a resolution to the issue that is affecting both parties in the business relationship. Finally, if no reasonable solution can be found or devised, your staff should be understanding and not degrading. After all, hard times don't last forever, and positive memories of their last collections call could ensure the lifetime loyalty of that customer.

All of these ideas result in customers who brag on 'their' insurance company, 'their' dry-cleaner, and 'their' tax preparer in the same way they brag on 'their' executive husband or 'their' graduate degree earning daughter. Once you have gotten to the point where even in tough times your customer wants sincerely to preserve and support the relationship, you may just find that appropriately addressing the collections issue with one customer increases sales volume from their word of mouth marketing.

Outbound (response or pre-emptive) issue resolution – Not every firm will actively employ this aspect of customer service. And of those that do, very few do so correctly. Established customer service centers will view this aspect as, "going the extra mile." This is unfortunate for the industries where this is an acceptable reality. However, it presents a unique opportunity for you to beat the hell out of your competition.

Your competitors will cheerfully pat themselves on the back for encouraging their CSRs to go the extra mile for the customer by identifying potential problems before they occur and seeking to address them. This sounds great, but what inevitably transpires is that CSRs also adopt the perspective that they are doing the customers a great big favor, completely unexpected and unrewarded. Too many times I have witnessed this positive facet of customer care be corrupted by a poorly managed business perspective. CSRs begin to resent the activity as a customer entitlement that steals time from other critical metrics like average call time or total calls per day.

Here's what this means for you:

Don't ever separate out out-bound issue resolution from the overall customer service strategy. Never treat this as an aspect separate from the overall care provided to your customers. Incorporate this type of service activity into the general training program. Exempt outbound call time from the standard metrics, or build new metrics around outbound customer service calls. Acknowledge and reward CSRs for their performance on outbound as well as on inbound service calls. Train representatives to anticipate future needs of the customers so they can make pre-emptive suggestions at the first customer contact; further reducing the need for additional outbound calls.

Once you change the dynamic regarding how this activity is viewed by your service assets, you will see service levels skyrocket. The final result of course, is a customer that feels like your representatives care more about his happiness in this business relationship than his favorite aunt feels about theirs.

General information – Self explanatory, right? This is when the customer just called in to ask a quick question or three. These types of customer interactions are actually the origin of all customer service, but in modern business general information calls have devolved into more of a business nuisance than an opportunity to service the customer.

Your competitors (in fact almost every business that can afford it) are spending loads of cash to automate the general information aspect of customer service. Customers who need general information tend to respond to automation in one of three ways:

1. They bypass it, resentfully
2. They use it, resentfully, or
3. They hang up and call back when they feel less resentful.

Automation of general information is fine for the internet and while the customer is holding for a representative. However, having a customer go through an unending stream of interactive prompts searching for one kernel of information is a certain way to lose positioning and possibly the customer altogether.

Here's what this means for you:

You will want to give your customer the option to get general info via a prompt system or press '0' to have their concerns addressed by the next available human being. That is, if you find investment in one of these automated information systems worth the money at all. I feel that they are best used for those who want to make a phone payment or ... well, just phone payments actually.

As I said earlier, keep the company address, payment address, fax number, etc. on the hold recording. But, if a customer calls to ask a question, let the customer ask a representative that will be able to build on the business relationship not a recorded voice that only builds resentment.

Supplementary services and product sales – More commonly referred to as "up-selling," this is traditionally viewed as an aspect of sales that is conveniently dumped on the customer service department. As such the average business manager factors an estimated sales potential into the expected revenues from the call center. At the same time, all of the CSRs pressured to become modern Fuller Brush Men develop a strong sense of resentment to the entire concept of "up-selling."

Your competitors won't even consider what it means to have a service representative who feels over pressured to sell additional goods and services to a customer calling with concerns about the goods and services they've already purchased. As the pressure to sell squeezes the ability to serve out of the available call time metric, even the most seasoned representatives will start to feel negatively about their job duties.

Here's what this means for you:

Manage the perspectives of your service staff. Remember, your talented customer care team doesn't want to be bogged down with sales duties; they want to focus their efforts, time and energies on making the customer happy with the company and their purchase. That doesn't mean that having your CSRs engage in up-selling is out of the question. What it means is that you should encourage your representatives to view up-selling as a tool to deliver more benefits and good feelings to your customers. Keep them from worrying about making sales, instead have them remain alert for opportunities to offer additional products and services that will address the customers' needs.

Any marginal decrease in revenue from supplemental sales per customer interaction will be more than offset by the increase in sales volume generated by the strengthening of the relationship with the customer and their faith in the fact that you actually want to serve their needs and not just sell them whatever you can get away with. You might also be surprised at the number of additional customer referrals you can generate just by this slight change in business perspective. Finally, the cake topper comes in the fact that you've improved morale among your staff by relieving pressure to sell and offering more tools to better do their jobs.

Refunds, returns and exchanges – I'm only willing to spend about three and a half minutes on this one, because it is ridiculous how many business managers and company leaders miss the boat on this aspect of customer service and how it can set a business apart and above its competitors.

Nobody wants to deal with Refunds, returns and exchanges; not managers, CSRs, and least of all customers. Unfortunately, it is an inevitability of doing business.

Your competitors will create a system that makes this process more convenient for purposes of tracking and accounting. For some unfathomable reason, business managers cannot make the connection between customer service and how these processes fit within the service mix. The overwhelming perspective is that the company should spend minimal effort on facilitating the giving back of any cash it's gained from sales.

Invariably, this attitude will translate into systems and procedures that make the processing of returns and refunds more difficult on CSRs and more disruptive and inconvenient for the customer. This is a potential relationship breaker every time a customer calls for this type of service.

Here's what this means for you:

Research and invest in a CRM software package or a proprietary system that streamlines the return, refund and exchange process for management, accounting, customer service and (most importantly) the customer. Educate your CSRs that this is a prime opportunity to retrieve market research regarding the origin of the customer's issue with your product or service. Use this customer interaction to empathize with the customer and find out how you can be of greater service in their next purchase. Remember, differentiation through customer service is ALL about relationship building. Even the best relationships have negative moments. However, if you recognize those negative moments as an opportunity to build trust and understanding while conveying a genuine sense of concern, you can convert those negatives into positives that will pay off ten-fold.

M. A. Sharrieff

Customer Service and Corporate Culture

Similar to every other aspect of your business structure, your customer service staff, department or division will be directly impacted by the culture of your organization. Corporate culture is not a culmination of the inputs of each individual working for the corporation, instead it is a gift or curse handed down from on high.

In the same way we inherited our ethnic culture from our parents and grandparents, the executive leadership, directors and other business leaders dictate what the personality of a corporate entity will be. The problem with this is that if your corporation has a culture that is negative, intransigent, and unsupportive, it is unlikely that anything done from middle management on down will change the situation.

Your competition will likely be made primarily of the culture types that have severely degraded over years of success. It is extremely rare to find an established market competitor that has maintained a culture that is flexible and responsive, considerate of internal and external customers, and aware of what role their culture plays in their ongoing success. More often, you will find that the established market forces have evolved a culture of entitlement and disdain for the necessity of customer service. After all, why should they care about the needs of the customer when they have all of this free-flowing success to wallow in, right?

Here's what this means for you:

If you've carved a niche in the market but you really want to beat the hell out of your competition, you'll need to analyze and refine your optimum corporate culture. Yes, your corporate culture can be engineered. However, the process will probably be as enjoyable as chewing a couple aspirin without a water chaser.

If you are a new market entrant, you have the advantage of establishing the optimum culture from the beginning of your enterprise. But, if you are reading this book, it is likely that you've already established yourself in the market, you are just nowhere near the head of the pack.

First, you need to understand the corporate cultures of your top three competitors. Since culture pervades every aspect of a business, you should not have to resort to corporate espionage to get some good research on these corporate personalities and the effects they have on their businesses.

Next, get all the leadership of your company to buy into the idea that an analysis and redirection of corporate culture can improve morale, boost sales, and make the business more competitive. These statements are all true, but it does gloss over the details of what will be involved in the process.

Then, and this is a really important step, don't trust yourself. Hire a change management or corporate culture consultant. Yes they do exist, and in a down economy they'll probably work for only five to 10% above whatever you think is reasonable (as opposed to 50% above reasonable in a booming economy). Let the professionals sell the business leadership on what behaviors they will have to alter in order to support a culture change in your business.

Now, how does customer service play into this strategy? Well, as I said earlier, your culture will literally soak through the behaviors, perspectives, and attitudes of every employee in your firm from the top down. Of course, this includes the customer service department as well. And this, my friend, is how you will communicate the superiority of your corporate culture in contrast to that of your competitors.

Remember, taking market share is like speed dating; you have about five minutes to make a better impression than the last guy did or the next guy will. Your customer service staff is the greatest tool to make that impression.

Another thing to remember is that the sales your business makes are the measurable results of the relationship your company is able to develop with the customer. So, as a business manager, you have to decide if you want the relationship to be a marriage or a one-night stand. In the case of the former, you can achieve a relationship that is mutually beneficial and can literally last generations. In the case of the latter, you might get that first sale, but you also might have to endure a certain amount of gossip about how less than satisfying the experience was for the customer.

As in any relationship, the customer is attracted by the product, the packaging, how conveniently things are delivered, and the reasonability of cost involved in getting into the relationship (remember our discussion on the 4 P's of marketing). However, just like interpersonal relationships, it is the personality of the prospective partner that will convince your target consumer to commit long-term. That personality is the corporations' culture and how that culture is communicated through every customer contact. Now, since 80% of all customer contacts will occur via customer service, it becomes obvious that selling your customer on a long-term business relationship depends on how well your customer service communicates your positive, attractive corporate culture.

Building Lifetime Customer Value

Now that you are no longer looking at customer interactions from a perspective of sales but one of long-term value derived from ongoing business relations, let's get closer to the true goal of any business relationship: Lifetime Customer Value.

Lifetime Customer Value (LCV) is one of those marketing terms that gets revised and regurgitated into the professional lexicon as a different variant every few years. But, since my own entry into the marketing industry almost 20 years ago, I haven't found a more descriptive term for what every company should be striving for in every single customer relationship.

Simply put, LCV denotes the value in sales and word of mouth promotion (or referrals) that a company derives from an individual customer over the entire length of the business relationship.

So, let's say that Customer A makes one sale with your company for $5,000 and then you never see that customer again. In contrast, Customer B makes one sale with your company every three months over a span of 10 years at only $100 per transaction.

Which of these two customers has a higher business value? Okay, not everybody is great at word problems, so I'll just tell you the answer: it all depends on how you define business value.

Your competition, shortsighted as they likely are, will define business value in terms of dollars per sale and/or total sales volume per transaction. Translation: 1) hold gun, 2) aim at foot, 3) pull trigger. These guys will look at the two customers described above and focus 80% of their business effort and marketing dollars at courting Customer A and customers just like him. While customers of this type do have their place, they fall into the 20% of your consumer population that will only generate periodic and marginal return on investment.

Here's what this means for you:

Your definition of business value must actually include the concept of value (how the relationship or interaction betters the current and future position of the company) as well as business (how much money the company just made).

If Customer A never makes another purchase, their lifetime value is the same as the business value of what $5,000 of revenue means to the company. However, the lifetime value of Customer B is the positive impact of $4,000 in revenue plus the impact of her positive word of mouth promotion of the company and brand to her friends and family, plus the referrals and additional business that are a direct result of that promotion.

So, Customer B has a greater LCV viewed through this perspective. And while your competitor spends his marketing dollar chasing Customer A for "flash-in-the-pan" profits, your business will center its efforts on Customer B who will then add value to the business relationship and profits to the company's bottom line, both directly and through promotion and referrals.

Now let's explore how your customer service department plays the critical part in how lifetime value is cultivated. Corporate trainers may teach your service staff to treat every customer the same, management and the standard operating procedures manual will likely echo this perspective. However, among the front-line grunts on your customer service floor there is a concept that is loosely recognized as A, B, C customer service.

The average representative will categorize each caller to determine how much time and attention the call merits. Customers that fall into category A will receive 80% of the CSR's time and effort. Customers in category B will receive 20%. And those that fall into category C? Well, let's just say that these calls are usually resolved, released or transferred within the first 90 seconds.

Now, as a business manager, I know that you are probably considering putting every one of your CSRs under Quality Assurance review to ensure this isn't happening on your call center floor. But before you put this book down and run off to your QA manager's office, just calm down and read a few more paragraphs.

The truth is that all CSRs in every call center practice A, B, C customer service. Hell, every person who picks up a telephone does the same thing. Within the first 20 seconds of a call, you yourself have made a determination of what category the caller falls into. Here's the trick though, as a manger, you have the ability to control the criteria your CSRs use to categorize each customer.

A lot of this criterion comes directly from the corporate culture. If emphasis is placed upon the importance of high dollar sales or total daily sales goals, your CSRs will place more importance on the Customer A type just to keep management off their backs. If importance is placed on building customer relationships, then the CSR will value the Customer B type who will make it clear in the first call that they are interested in an ongoing business relationship. So, it becomes critical that you educate your service staff to where they can find the greatest value for the company and reward them when they achieve that value.

Once your service staff understands that Customer B types should be categorized so they receive Class-A customer service and Customer A types should get Class-B service instead of the other way around, you'll be astounded at how quickly sales volumes through the service center increase. First, the number of long-term customers will increase as they refer customers with similar service expectations. Second, the population of one-time purchasers will be serviced more effectively and efficiently since you are now only dedicating 20% of your service time and marketing dollars toward these customers.

What's really crazy and often overlooked is that the Type A customers are usually the customers who don't want to stay on the phone being up-sold, catered to or receive any ancillary attention. They usually just want to have their problem solved and get on with their life.

So, we'll just let your competition waste time and money improperly servicing their customers while you keep your service staff focused on giving the right level of service to those customers who find the most value in it.

Oh, and don't worry about category C customer service. If you stay on track with the suggestions above and elsewhere in this book, the only calls that should fall into the C category are crank calls, wrong numbers and callers trying to be transferred from customer service to executive management (usually hoping to sell something).

Generating New Sales through Customer Service

Well, assuming that you've read straight through, you know from the previous sections that customer service stimulates new business primarily through customer referrals. You've also gained a perspective on how your customer service representatives do 100% of the heavy lifting when it comes to solving the problems and delivering the good feelings that will keep customers bringing their friends, family and business associations to your company's door.

Now, I'm going to jump back into marketing to give a little perspective of what passes for the standard method of attracting new sales in the American business world. Most marketing professionals, regardless of the industry will advocate for a marketing mix that is weighted heavily toward promotion and advertising. Next in line are public relations campaigns. Then, if the industry is accepting of it, marketers will still consider direct marketing (which used to be just mail-outs, but today includes email and text marketing, etc.).

As a business manager or business executive, you may not have a clear understanding as to why this is the standard even across different industries. Well, to let you in on a long held business secret, promotion and ad campaigns are the most fun and direct marketing campaigns are a bore. Marketers also like to get a lot of attention for their efforts. There just isn't a lot of buzz involved in a texting blitz. But a new commercial is something worth notice.

Now I don't want you to think that professionalism doesn't exist in the marketing industry. It absolutely does. However, it is worth recognizing that one aspect of marketing doesn't even make the list. Yes, that's right, customer service.

If marketing is communicating solutions and good feelings to your customers, then why do marketers regularly overlook the most direct, controllable, cost effective, measurable, and efficient channel of marketing communication available?

Same reason why you did, they hadn't read this book yet!

Absolutely none of your competitors (that have not already read this book) will have the necessary insight to recognize their customer service division for the marketing resource that it could be. They will undoubtedly continue to follow the marketing standard and continue to receive their industries' standard for marketing returns on investment.

Here's what this means for you:

You have an incredible opportunity to beat the hell out of your competition by insisting that your marketing team design a promotional strategy that includes your customer service department. This could include referral competitions, customer promotions exclusively available through the customer care center, or any number of marketing campaign ideas. What becomes critical is that the promotion should lend itself to the position of the customer service representative as the customer's direct contact with the company and all those lovely solutions and good feelings they undoubtedly want to share with as many referrals as possible. Reward the customer's participation, reward the CSR's participation, deliver on the promotion and then, when you measure the results, you'll find that not only have you gotten a greater return on your marketing dollar invested but you spent less marketing dollars delivering on this campaign than other, less measurable marketing efforts.

Getting a bigger bang for your marketing buck is a certain way to beat the hell out of your competition over the long haul. And your customer service department is the easily accessible vehicle that will get you there.

M. A. Sharrieff

Customer Complaints as Business Opportunities

It's no secret that customers complain. And everybody knows that those complaints are gold mines of information letting you know how to better your product and service offerings. Complaints help to identify and address the needs of existing customers and generate new business through referrals. In fact, the original reason for the establishment of organized customer service departments was to address customer complaints.

Of course, back in those days the driving force behind having a customer call the "complaints department" was to keep customers from abusing the time of the all important sales department. Well, despite the fact that everyone in the modern business world knows that this is an outdated and backward perspective, it never fails to amaze me just how many business leaders still feel this way. Many still feel that complaints are to be fielded by customer service staff trained to placate customers (within a certain financial limit, of course) and get rid of any customers unreasonable enough to fall outside the established range of reasonability.

I know this really sounds like a cynical view. However, what you have to understand is that it is basic human nature to want to distance yourself from negativity. This fact of human psychology translates to the larger corporate body as well. After all, as Massachusetts Governor, Mitt Romney famously said, "Corporations are people, too."

So, while politically I think Romney was a little off base, in the context of what we're discussing here, he was right on target. It's a little like squeezing one apple or a whole truck load; despite the differences, the juice tastes pretty much the same.

This means that your competitors who will likely not have this insight into human nature will allow their customer service department to evolve into a daily expression of the natural human reaction to forced exposure to negativity. And it isn't positive.

Think about it. Maybe you've been at a restaurant and the jerk at the next table decides to really let their server have it because his steak wasn't cooked just right. Or, maybe you've been in line at the grocery and the person in front of you starts making angry comments about the elderly customer writing a check for their purchase or the clerk who needs to call for assistance. How did you feel? Even if you agreed with the person's position, I'm sure their behavior and attitude didn't give you a warm fuzzy feeling.

No one wants to wait longer than what they consider reasonable, or receive what they consider bad service. A certain amount of disappointment and frustration in these circumstances is more than understandable. However, the natural response to an overly negative reaction is to want to leave the situation, to feel nervous and uncomfortable. In some circumstances, we even find it hard to resist the urge to strike back against an undeserved attack or the inappropriate attacker.

Think about this scenario: you are the wait staff, you've provided great service but this customer has just called into question your professional competence, intelligence and parentage because the meal he ordered wasn't as anticipated. You didn't prepare the meal, but since you laid it before him you get to receive the brunt of his tirade.

So how do you respond? Well, if you want to keep your job, you attempt to placate the customer. You apologize slavishly, and you wait until the end of your shift to voice how you really feel about the experience.

Your competitors will have completely missed the point of the scenario above, but here's the quick and dirty. The wait staff IS your customer service staff. That jerk of a customer will be on the other end of 20% of all of your inbound calls (certain industries like finance and medical services might see as high as 80%).

Now, the big question is what is missing from this customer service interaction?

If you said the customer service, then I know you've gotten some value out of the previous sections.

But how can we be missing the customer service since the customer received an apology, maybe a new meal (that may or may not have been spit in) and possibly a discount on his next meal, surely that customers' complaints have been adequately addressed and customer service has been delivered?

Unfortunately, all that has occurred in the above scene is the rewarding of bad behavior. I'm not saying that the apology should not have been given or any of the accommodations offered, if the accommodations are appropriate. What I am saying is that if the root of the customer's complaint was the preparation of the food then (despite the customer's negativity) the server needs to discern that, relay the information to management so that corrections can be made for the benefit of this and every other customer as well.

In addition, customer service means controlling the interaction to an extent that the customer understands that the outcome of their complaint depends upon the cooperative effort of the customer and the service representative against the problem; not the company, not the management, and certainly not the service representative.

Finally, the server needs to understand that part of their job is to rise above the natural response to negativity dictated by human psychology and focus not on the complainer, but on the complaint. This is a skill that, once developed, provides the representative with the power to productively manage the entirety of the service interaction regardless of the disposition of the customer.

Here's what this means for you:

The tendency your competition will have toward allowing the disposition of their customer service to be dictated by the natural response to negativity will result in an exploitable competitive weakness you can use to beat the hell out of them. Not deriving the valuable intelligence necessary to improve their business processes, product and service offerings, and the customer experience will offer you the opportunity to steal their market share by doing what they aren't.

As a manager, you'll need to constantly evaluate the attitude and departmental culture of your customer service department. You will need to regularly interject positivity and manage the perspective of your service staff so they remember that addressing a customer complaint is not the entirety of customer service. Ensure that your staff has the training and support necessary for them to effectively control the interaction, ally themselves with the customer to combat the problem and create wins for the customer, the company, and themselves.

When you analyze your customer's experiences compared to those of your competitors', you will see the marked difference that explains your increasing market share and customer good will.

Maximizing Human Capital

If you've read this book straight through, then you know that I am not the biggest fan of customer service via auto response prompt systems. Regardless of how pleasant the recorded operator is, the best customer service is an interactive experience between a live customer and a live service representative. I strongly believe that despite technological advances, the live customer service representative is a difficult position to automate without significant sacrifice to your business position.

As a result, management will always be tasked with the recruitment, training, development and retention of human capital. Again, we find a perspective in need of management. Despite what is advertised, most call centers significantly devalue their customer service staff. It varies greatly, but I have been exposed to attitudes ranging from. "I give them all the training and software they need to service our customers, they shouldn't need anything else." to, "Any monkey can answer a phone."

Though I have encountered training programs, staff management, corporate culture, and Customer Relationship Management (CRM) packages that have been incredible and those that have been less than passable, I have yet to see a staff management program comprehensive enough to maximize the value of an entities' service staff. All too often I see organizations that focus on only one aspect of the staff management mix while ignoring other necessary facets. Even worse is the tendency to not do such a great job on the area they decide to focus on.

Okay, let's take a minute to break down the staff management mix for those who may be unfamiliar with the term. Similar to the marketing mix we discussed earlier, the staff management mix has four primary aspects:

1. Recruitment and training
2. Environment and culture
3. Resources
4. Development

This is where the similarities end. While marketing concerns itself with communication, when managing human resources you actually have to deliver something!

Think of it like this, whenever business leadership seeks to fill a position; they are looking to make a business transaction. Management wants a task performed and they are willing to pay a certain number of dollars in exchange. Of course, like most things in the business world, this is a vast oversimplification. Fortunately for you, most of your competitors will still be thinking of the management-labor relationship in these terms.

Instead, modern management of human assets requires that you address all four areas of staff management in order to maximize your return on investment (ROI).

Let's cover the four areas in brief:

Recruitment and Training – A great deal of your success in staff management is tied into your initial selection and training of your customer service team. It will be your responsibility to understand your corporate culture and if the applicant can work well within it. You will need to understand how your customers need to be served and if the applicant has the "soft skills" (person-ability, tenacity, poise, etc.) necessary for your company and industry, and if you and your customers will be able to rely on them to consistently deliver. Find a good fit between position, company, and applicant and you are more than halfway there.

Never feel bad about not hiring an applicant that doesn't seem to fit in some way, even if they are the most delightful interview you've ever had in your life. Customer service is a tough job (that's why you're in management and not answering the phones yourself). A poorly placed customer service representative creates a "lose, lose, lose" proposition. Customers will not get outstanding service, the representative will be consistently unhappy, and you will eventually have to terminate them anyway (wasting the recruitment and training investment you put into the representative).

Once you have found an applicant that is compatible with the position and the company, you will need to deliver a superior training program that comprehensively prepares the applicant to provide outstanding customer service when they first interact with your customer. Too many managers and corporate trainers focus solely on systems training without conveying a holistic understanding of who their customer is, what they expect, and how their needs should be addressed. Your representatives need to have a clear understanding of what support they can expect from their direct supervisors and the rest of the management staff, what strategies and best practices exist, and exactly how empowered they are to find solutions to your customers problems.

In addition to all this, make sure they know how to use the phone system, too!

Environment and culture – I want to reiterate that customer service is a tough job. It isn't the highest paid business profession despite its necessity and too often the efforts of service representatives go unnoticed and under-appreciated. Customer service as a profession bears an attrition rate similar to (and in some industries, higher than) the fast food industry. And it is very rare to find a professional customer service representative who has an average longevity rate of more than 30 months.

While this might give a less than attractive air to the customer service position, the customer service professional overall really loves their job.

Well, if they love their job, why the high attrition, why the "job-hopping" every two – three years, right?

Even though professional customer service representatives genuinely love what they do, all too often the hate where they do it.

The biggest causes of CSR disgruntlement:

1. Stagnation – "I've got no opportunity to advance here." And, "I haven't had a raise in two years."

2. Under-appreciation - "No matter how hard I work, nobody cares."

3. Lack of Empowerment -"Why won't they just let me do my job?" And, "I'd be a lot more successful at my job if they wouldn't tie my hands."

4. Lack of Leadership -"My boss doesn't even understand what I do for this company."And, "My boss only cares about metrics."

5. Disrespect - "Working in customer service is like being counted as three-fifths of a person."

These attitudes are experienced by the majority of customer service representatives throughout the industry. It becomes your duty as a manager or business leader to create the kind of environment that can actively combat these sentiments.

The first, best step you can take toward this goal is to understand that the modern customer service professional is one part Concierge, one part Social Service Professional, and one part Au

Pair. The only reason anyone stays in the customer service industry is because it provides them a method to be of service to others. Unfortunately, like so many other professional caregivers, their value to their employers is often overlooked or undervalued.

The second step toward creating an environment where your CSRs are anxious to come to work and make you money is to understand that the nature of a caregiver is emotionally based. This means that money is not always the answer. Okay, so let's be real, if you don't pay your talent appropriately you'll find yourself with a high attrition rate and competitors who are continually stealing the human resources you've invested time, treasure and training in.

Beyond competitive salaries, you need to appreciate the human beings that are helping your customer understand the value in doing business with you. This could mean a birthday card signed by the CEO, a gift card to recognize achievements in sales, service, attendance, or the receipt of a significant customer compliment. You should feel free and comfortable keeping these displays of recognition simple yet sincere. If your team leads, supervisors and management staff are doing their jobs, they'll have no choice but to know something about the interests and motivations of their subordinates.

Use these motivations to guide the activities and acknowledgements you design for your CSRs. Keep in mind that these are not faceless positions, but sensitive individuals. In fact, your topmost performers will be the most empathetic and the most sensitive. You will get a surprising amount of loyalty and service from these professionals with a few genuine gestures of appreciation.

Here's a third step to success in caring for your customer care team: Promote from within!

It is astounding how many businesses extol this as a virtue, and then forget to practice it. Ensure that ALL of your customer service team leads have spent time on your customer service floor as a representative. Call center supervisors, trainers, and managers should have experience serving your company and its customers as a representative.

I know many business leaders will advocate for a professional outside hire for supervisors and managers of their call centers. After all, their representatives know the phones and won't have the necessary skill-sets to manage others.

There are two blaring problems with this strategy from a purely business perspective.

1. Your externally sourced manager will cost you additional time resources necessary to learn your company, product, market, and customer care staff.

2. You will experience a predictable and costly drop in service levels floor wide as morale drops in response to your, "bringing an outsider into the family." Remember, if you have been successful in hiring the best CSRs, you will have a talented group of professionals that are motivated by emotional stimulus. The reaction of having an unknown element thrust upon them will almost always be met with fear and anxiety; which translates into reduced productivity.

You will undoubtedly find yourself better served by having the best candidate trained to be a manager than trying to have a manager train to understand the internal dynamic of your call center and its members. In addition, you now have installed leadership that knows the job and the employees they must direct. Your service staff will respect experience and go further to support a leader that comes from within the ranks.

Finally, change the paradigm that customer service is the department everyone wants to get away from. Promoting leadership from the call center floor will help spread a sense of professional self respect within the department. However, to inspire a feeling that the customer service environment is a positive one, post the accomplishments and customer compliments of your call center staff where other departments can see them. Direct company tours through your call center floor, acknowledging the superiority of your service staff. Include the CSRs on the invite list for the company Christmas party, picnic or softball league. You will be astounded by the mileage you get simply by not treating the customer service center like the corporate stepchild.

Resources – Once you have recruited an exemplary service staff, trained them to provide world-class customer service and designed an environment that makes them eager to come to work each day, the absolute worst thing you could do to frustrate your efforts is to not offer your CSRs the necessary tools to do the job they are so passionate and eager to do.

Before you put down this book and rush off to count your phones and computer stations, I want to clarify what I mean by the term "tools."

In the jargon of the customer service industry, the term "tools" refers to absolutely anything that facilitates the ability of the representative to satisfactorily address the business concerns of both the customer and the company.

This is going to include tangible tools like equipment and software, internet access and vendor contact sheets as well as intangible tools like the ability to offer certain accommodations and access certain processes to find the "best right answer" to the customer's problem while ensuring long-term profitability for their employer.

Your CSRs should feel adequately empowered to make certain, reasonable accommodations that will help them achieve that best right answer. They should also understand the limits of reasonability and have the confidence that escalation of any customer issue will be treated with the same passion for finding the best right answer that the representative originally approached the issue with.

To be even more succinct; don't tie the hands of your CSRs, and when they have exhausted the limits of their toolbox, they should have managerial resources that feel just as willing to partner with the customer against the problem as the CSR does.

It's important to remember that just as you want the customer to think of you as "their" business resource, your best customer service professionals will think in terms of "their" company and "their" customers. This is exactly where you want them to be! But, once you have them there, don't frustrate their efforts by not appearing to share their attitude toward being the hero for the company and the customer.

Development – This area of the staff management mix is the most often overlooked in customer service centers everywhere. We'll need to start by shifting the managerial perspective of what professional development means within the realm of customer service.

The commonly held understanding of what it means to develop human assets within the customer care environment is synonymous with training. Furthermore, the training is for the current position of Customer Service Representative exclusively. Of course, in those rare instances where management improves processes or implements new software or technology, it may be necessary to further 'develop' their customer service staff.

Hopefully this is a belief only held by your competition and not by you. This paradigm is the greatest cause of staff apathy within any given service center. Remember, customer care professionals are emotionally motivated. When you educate them to the fact that you only care that they are in their seats and answering phones, many will commit to that and only that.

In contrast, the call center that develops career path programs, training and development programs that reach throughout the call center and into the greater body of the business; these call centers see incredibly low attrition rates, high performance metrics and consistently high morale. Why? Because the service staff feels that you have an interest in their career, and that you want to help them be a better employee and give them opportunities to be of greater service to the company and its customers.

There will be business leaders who will argue that it makes no sense to take a top performing customer care representative and develop them so they promote out to the accounting department. Why not? The accountants who service your company have customers. These customers may be internal; the production department, human resources, or management of any internal department. They may also service external customers; the IRS, corporate vendors, or the accounts payable departments of other businesses you trade with.

Doesn't it make sense to install a professional into the position that knows your company, product, clientele, and knows how to interact with both internal and external customers to get results? And if this holds true for an accounting position, it's even more valid for positions in management, production and sales. Of course you'll want to ensure these CSRs have the necessary training to leverage their current skill sets into greater efficiency and profitability for your firm. To accomplish this you will need to have two basic things:

1. A proactive, forward thinking approach to your business growth strategy and,

2. A commitment to optimizing your human assets to the betterment of your bottom line

I'll bet you thought I was going to get all mushy and altruistic about doing the right thing by your staff and the warm fuzzy feelings it would bring. But the truth is this type of business strategy is completely focused on profitability. In the same way it costs more to develop an outside CSR manager than promoting a CSR to management after developing their management skills, the total cost of training a CSR for almost any position is less than that of an outside hire trained in the discipline but ignorant of your company.

Of course, I am not advocating that you promote a service representative to a position as an accounting manager without the candidate having the necessary knowledge and skills, but once they've achieved their accounting and/or management degree, is keeping them on the call center floor completely appropriate? The challenge is for you to work out reasonable paths of advancement that benefit your organization consistently over the long term and continuously develop the value of the staff member on that path. Here's what this means for you:

Creating a development program that starts at your customer service floor will guarantee you a stable pool of willing and ready talent that is as enthusiastic about the company's success as its founders. These employees will have a greater degree of loyalty for the company and a higher level of performance at every position they are posted in. Once you educate them that the company cares about them, they will feel the need care about the company.

The knowledge that being a customer service representative is the start of a career and not just a dead end job will boost morale and you will constantly have employees striving to prove their value in order to have that value developed to the next achievable level. Eventually, your development effort will result in a corporate body that is passionate about the vision and mission of your firm. All of this translates to greater profitability as your business achieves growth through the increased effectiveness of its human resources.

Customer Service Driven Growth Strategies

Some readers might have picked up this book and been overwhelmingly tempted to go straight to this section thinking it would contain a succinct listing of how to use customer service to grow their market share. Well, the good news is that this section will offer some input on how to do just that. The bad news, depending on how you look at it, is that all of the other sections also offer information on how strategic use of your customer service assets will grow your business. So, if you did skip ahead to this section, it's alright to continue. However, you should be prepared to go back and read the rest of the book to get the full value I'm offering. You won't be disappointed.

Similar to the previous sections, I want to start by identifying poor perspectives and then we'll move on to understanding why and how you can change them in order to benefit your company.

These days, it is incredibly difficult to differentiate one company's market offering from that of a competitor. When grouped by price point (i.e. low cost, mid-range, or premium priced), products and service offerings become relatively homogeneous. Those companies determined not to end up scrabbling for any portion of market share with a host of competitors who look just like them are gaining an awareness of the power of customer service.

We've already discussed how you can use customer service to market your brand, but to really achieve growth, you'll need to weave customer service into your brand. In the mind of your target consumer, placing a call or any contact with your business should be because they are seeking superior customer service and the fact that you make the best widgets for the price is just a happy coincidence.

Too often entrepreneurs are fooled by early success. Armed with passion and good ideas, an entrepreneur enters the market ready to combat his competition with improved products, processes, pricing strategies, or other business efficiencies. If the new business is lucky, they capture the attention of enough of their target market and carve out a piece of the pie.

These lucky ones revel in their success and plan to grow their market with new ads, promotional discounts, sales and gimmicks. Unfortunately, with every other market participant doing exactly the same thing, these new companies just end up adding to the background noise. Customers having to filter through all this background noise no longer look at the upstart company as a new and better solution to their problems, but instead your company has become one of a number of suitable substitutes within a large solution set.

You want that customer's business, but not just because they happened to be on your side of the street that day. You want your potential customer to look at your brand and regard it as the only reasonable option to address their consumer need.

Here's how you can do that. All consumer behaviorists know that the purchase decision is based on their perception of how well a vendor can address their need at any given time. For example, a consumer might make a particular purchase regularly at four o'clock every Saturday afternoon. With all things being equal, that consumer is more likely to patronize a vendor that stays open until six o'clock, versus a vendor that closes at four-thirty. Why? Well, (all other factors being equal) in the mind of the consumer, the possibility that there might be a circumstance that would require a late purchase would make the six o'clock vendor the obvious choice. Here, the service of additional time to make the purchase has won the customer.

Here's what this means for you:

When you have defined your target consumer, ensure that your definition includes an accurate depiction of their customer service needs and expectations. Once you have these expectations defined, exceed them consistently. Define your brand image by your customer service. Market the idea that solving your customer's problems and providing them with good feelings in the process is your corporate mission and vision. Define your business success by how satisfied your customers are with your service and not by how many units you sell and you'll be astounded at how many more units you will sell.

Once your target consumer has clearly positioned your brand as the solutions and good feelings provider within your market, that position becomes yours to lose, and no competitor will be able to take that from you.

Customer Service Trends

The concept of customer service has existed in modern business for a very long time. During that time, there have been many trends regarding how customers should be serviced, what tools and implementation strategies should be used.

As a business leader, you owe it to your firm not to get caught up in the trends without giving them the necessary consideration. Also, you owe it to your service staff to provide them with the best and most appropriate tools to do their jobs. Finally, you have a duty to your customers to offer high quality service in the most effective and efficient manner possible. Think of it as a scale with three arms. Once you have balanced the needs of your staff, your company, and your consumer, any trends that have not been eliminated should be considered for implementation.

Some time ago there was a dramatic market trend toward outsourcing the customer service function to developing third-world countries. After that, there was a major move to implement customer relationship management (CRM) software in hopes that many of the customer service functions could benefit from automated tracking and record keeping. There was a trend in automating telephone customer service, moving customer service functions online to "self-service" corporate websites, customer service via email, and lately, customer service via live chat and text message.

Some of these trends have proven to be reinvigorating to the business potential and service capabilities of certain business entities, while others have proven the disastrous downfall of a number of firms. Like many other trends that I didn't list and those that are just over the horizon, none are inherently right or wrong. What you will need to ask yourself is whether or not any current or upcoming trend in customer service is the "best" right answer for my business, my customers and my staff.

Far too many businesses spent millions on severance and unemployment compensation, relocation costs and the recruitment and training of new staff after outsourcing their customer services to China and India only to spend more to "in-source" those functions back into the domestic markets.

M. A. Sharrieff

For some companies designed around e-commerce, it makes complete sense to build customer service into their sites; not only will their customer base expect it, but they prefer it. In contrast, firms in the jewelry, high fashion or skilled services industries have wasted untold amounts of cash when their customers demand one-on-one, interpersonal customer service.

Here's what this means for you:

Your detailed knowledge of your service assets' capacity, your business' needs and your customers' expectations will offer you a competitive advantage when evaluating the continuing influx of customer service trends. While your competitors flounder between options, haphazardly selecting whatever new idea sounds good, you can take a laser focus on those ideas that make the most sense and translate into the most dollars.

~~***~~

Conclusion

Okay, boys and girls, so what have we learned today? No need to raise your hands, just shout out your answer.

First, Customer Service should be a potent facet of your marketing and business strategy. Second, it is a powerful tool to advance your business toward success in your industry. And, third, it is likely that nine out of ten of your competitors refuse to acknowledge the potential market advantages that a strong customer service based business model can deliver.

These are the foundational points I want you to take from this book. But I'll take a second to distill the major topics we've discussed in this volume.

1. Customer service as a marketing tool – your customers are exposed to your brand through your customer service staff every day, don't fail to take advantage of the free marketing potential your CSRs and customer service assets can provide.

2. Obtaining Market Research through Customer Service – Every business needs qualified market intelligence, and it is usually very expensive to obtain. If only there was a way that your business could get this information directly from the customer without breaking the bank. Oh, wait, there is!

3. Differentiation through Customer Service – Every customer in your market wants to be treated better. Once your firm is known for treating its customers better than any of your competitors, you might find that you are alone in a market with all of the customers and your competition exist in a different market entirely (with customers who don't like superior service).

4. Customer Service and Corporate Culture – The strength of your firm is dictated by the integrity of its corporate culture. A negative corporate culture will damage the effectiveness of your customer service. Manage your firm's culture with this in mind and you'll see your customer service productivity skyrocket!

5. Building Lifetime Customer Value – Customers are only interested in solutions to problems and good feelings, and they only want that at every single point of contact! After the sale, your customer service assets will be the primary means of proving your commitment and consistency to your customer. Maximizing this

aspect of your customer service strategy can turn a modest sale into a lifetime of continual purchases and referrals.

6. Generating New Sales through Customer service – Do you want your friends mad at you because you sent them to a vendor that offered them poor solutions and bad feelings? Well, neither do your customers. Treat them better than they expect and they'll bring friends and family to you by the dozens.

7. Customer Complaints as Business Opportunities – When a customer complains, they are telling you they want to do business with you and, as soon as you can remove a particular impediment, they would be happy to give you money. If the issue can be reasonably resolved you can be confident that you have improved your brand's position in the mind of the complaining customer and all the hundreds of other customers who don't complain (you know, the customers just take their business to your competitor).

8. Maximizing Human Capital – Your customer service team can be the "ringer" when going head to head with your market competitors. However, if you refuse to train, support and encourage the best from your customer care staff, you may as well not have customer service at all. Poorly developed human capital can do real damage to your firm's competitive position.

9. Customer Service driven growth strategies - Define your growth strategies based upon the needs of your customer not the needs of your business. Focus on the implementation of tactics that will achieve greater market access by delivering higher standards of service to the customer. Ensure that the service(s) you provide are the ones that bring enhanced value and your customer base and market share will grow incredibly.

10. Customer Service Trends - Understand that new trends in customer service will hit the business scene every 12 – 18 months, and old ones will be considered out of date in the same time period. What you need to focus on is the fact that whatever trend looks attractive to you must be analyzed based on the value it can deliver to your firm, your customer, and your customer care staff. Any trend that doesn't provide increased, balanced value in all three areas should be discarded like junk mail.

So, those are the crib notes. It's my hope that you'll read through this book several times; at least one of those times, with a pencil and paper as you redefine your marketing and business strategies to include a greater customer service dynamic. Remember to be diligent in your development of your customer service assets, because let's face it, some of your competitor's can read, too!

Cheers!

~M. A. Sharrieff

~~###~~

More about the Author

Malik Sharrieff is a single father of two young sons and currently resides between Cedar Hill, Texas and New Orleans, Louisiana. In addition to writing on topics of business development, Malik is also working on several short works of contemporary fiction, fantasy and science fiction that will be profiled in several upcoming anthologies published by Write On E-Publishing, LLC. If you've enjoyed this title, please look for other works by this author.
Thank you!

Discover more titles from this author and Write On E-Publishing at www.WriteOnPress.com, www.Amazon.com
or
Your favorite digital or print book retailer

Other Write On Press titles that you might enjoy featuring this author:

Endings & Beginnings
M. A. Sharrieff,
David Hale
&
H. C. Heartland

www.ingramcontent.com/pod-product-compliance
Lightning Source LLC
Chambersburg PA
CBHW071647170526
45166CB00003B/1473